IT'S A COLD TODAY, JANE

by Nettie Lowenstein

Pictures by Doffy Weir

"It's a cold day today, Jane," said Jane's mother, as Jane was getting dressed for school.
"It's a very cold day."

"You'd better wear your warm brown dress with the long sleeves."

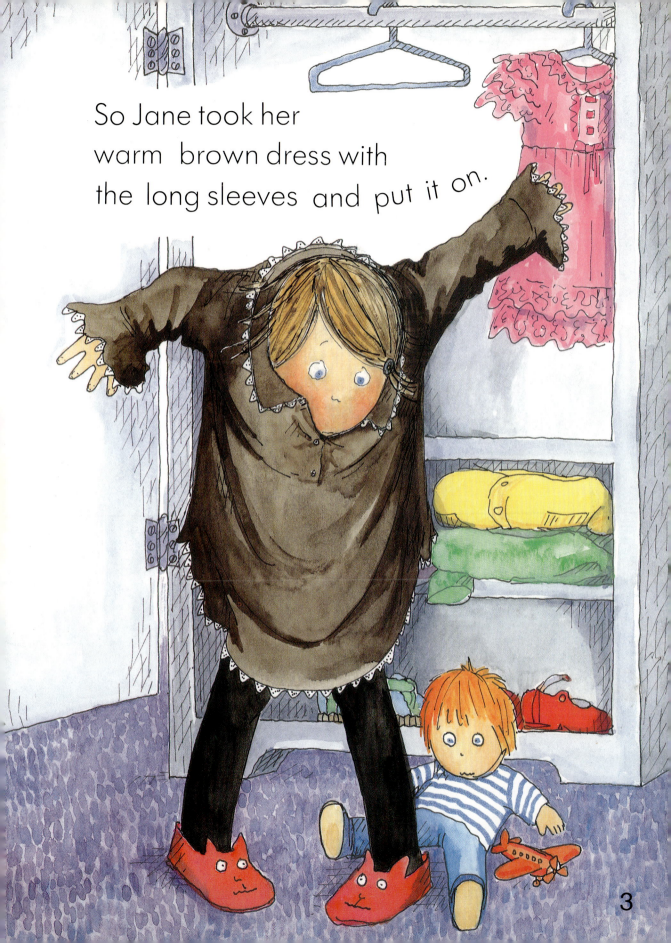

So Jane took her warm brown dress with the long sleeves and put it on.

"It's a cold day today, Jane," said Jane's mother, as she opened the back door and let in the cat. "It's a really cold day."

"You'd better wear your yellow cardigan, the one your Nan knitted you last Christmas."

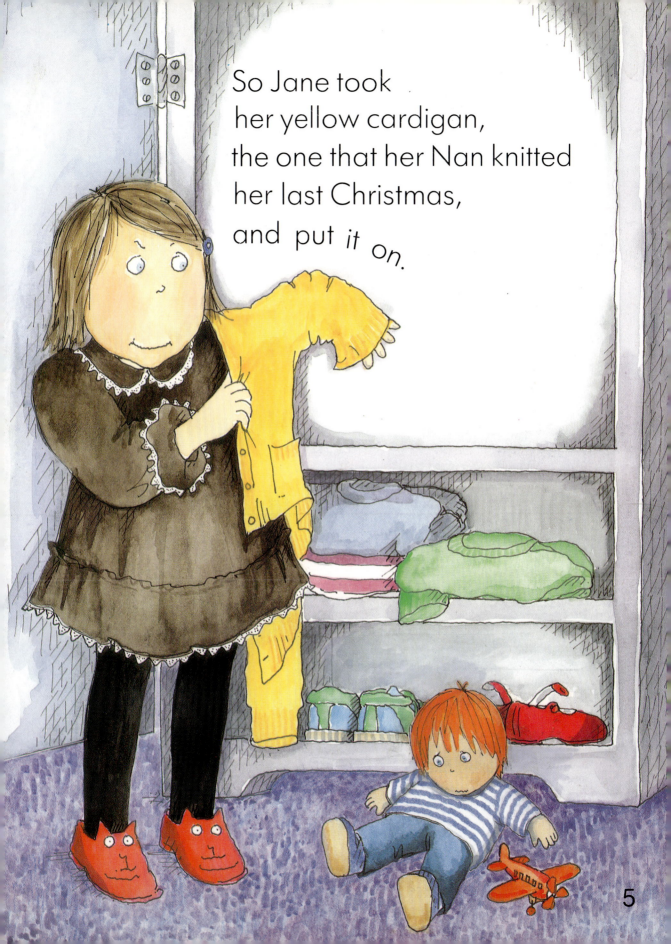

So Jane took her yellow cardigan, the one that her Nan knitted her last Christmas, and put it on.

"It's a cold day today, Jane," said Jane's mother, as she answered the front door bell and took in a parcel from the postman. "It's a dreadfully cold day."

"You'd better wear your wool-lined boots and your warm winter coat."

So Jane took her wool-lined boots and her warm winter coat and put them on.

"It's a cold day today, Jane," said Jane's mother, as she stood at the front door ready to take Jane to school.
"It's a freezing cold day."

"You'd better wear your scarf and your woolly hat, and don't forget your gloves."

So Jane took her scarf and her woolly hat and she didn't forget her gloves and she put them on.

And now, at last,
Jane was ready for school.

"We'll have to hurry," said Jane's mother, "or we'll be late."

They hurried across the road. And they hurried down the next street.

And as they hurried
the sun came out,
and it shone, and it shone,
and it wasn't cold at all.
In fact, it was warm.

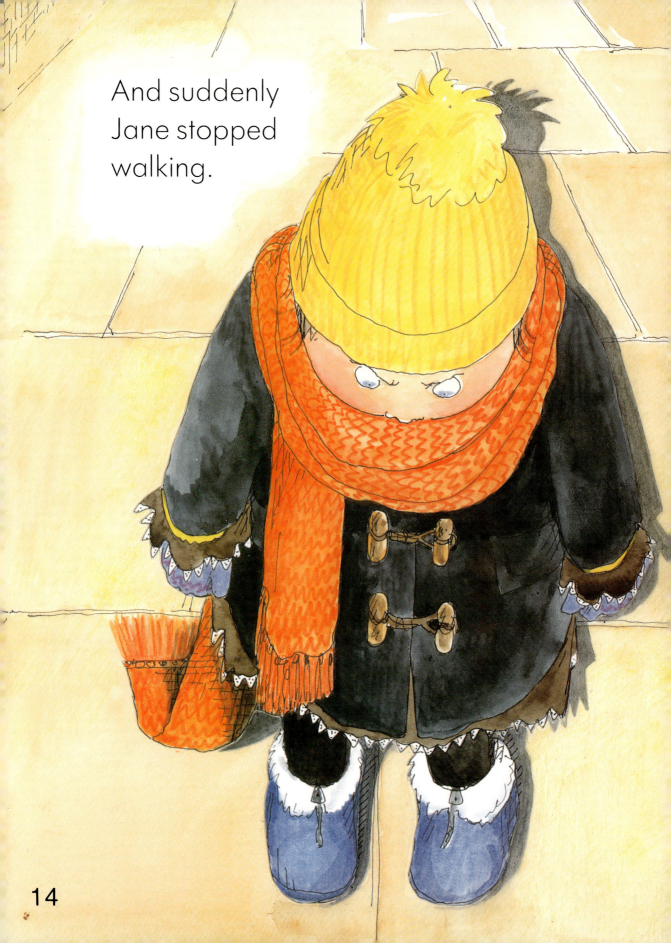
And suddenly Jane stopped walking.

She stood
in her scarf,
and her gloves,
and her warm woolly hat,
and her wool-lined boots,
and her warm winter coat,
and her warm brown dress,
and her yellow cardigan,
the one her Nan knitted her
last Christmas.
And she wouldn't move at all.

"Come on," said Jane's mother.
"I can't," said Jane.
"I can't go on."

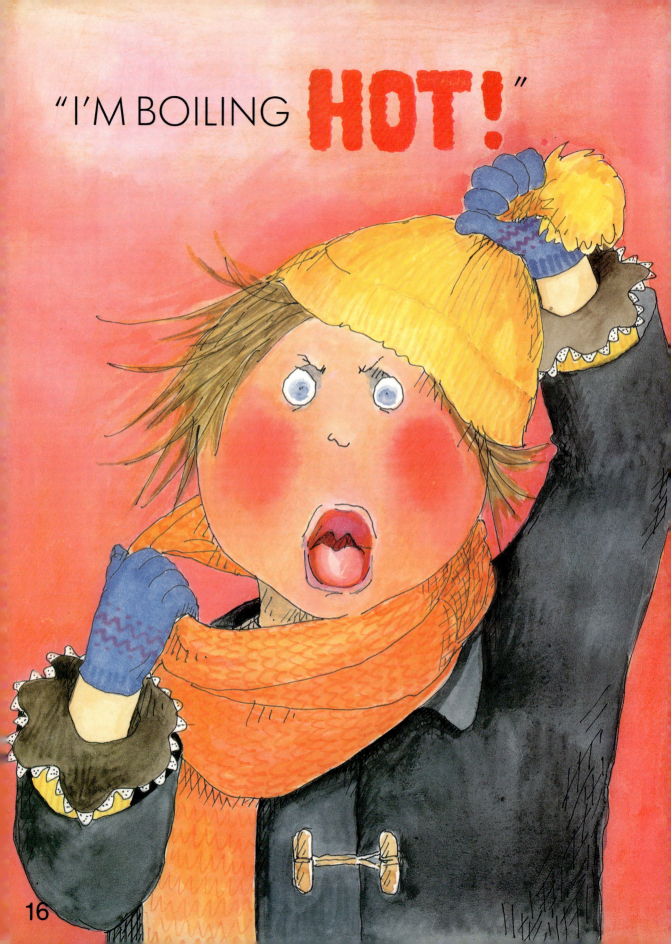